creative direction & design vertical designs
cover photo guildhaus photographics
chapter photos kelley styring
chapter illustrations vertical designs
original product concepts kelley styring
product illustrations geoff marko, brandhouse inc.

IN YOUR PURSE

Archaeology of the American Handbag

A catalyst *for* innovation.

AuthorHouse™
1663 Liberty Drive, Suite 200
Bloomington, IN 47403
www.authorhouse.com
Phone: 1-800-839-8640

First published by AuthorHouse 7/3/2007

ISBN: 978-1-4343-1706-3 (sc)

Library of Congress Control Number: 2007904859

Printed in the United States of America
Bloomington, Indiana

This book is printed on acid-free paper.

authorHOUSE®

thanks.

This book is dedicated to women who slog through life with three pounds on their shoulders every day. Because in those three pounds they carry the weight of their responsibility for themselves, for others, and for how their world turns around them.

Special thanks to Steve, Collin, Gillian, and Papa, for making my world turn while I did this study. Thanks to Bill, Alice, Heather and Judi for blocking & tackling. And thanks to Mark, Sandi, Debbie, Tom, and Aditi for making it all look easy. I couldn't have done it without you.

table of contents.

preface.

epilogue.

The Meticulous Dig

Throughout history, explorers have pushed our boundaries, expanding our world from what is known into what is possible. Some, like Magellan, mapped uncharted regions of the Earth. Others like John Glenn, gave us a glimpse of the heavens. Da Vinci gave us our first look at the internal workings of the human body. Freud plumbed the depths of the human mind.

Brave men, one and all, but I think they'd shudder in their boots at my meticulous dig — "In Your Purse: Archaeology of the American Handbag." One hundred women, 2 cities, 11 days of digging into purse after purse to reveal its stomach contents down to the last snotty tissue and connecting what was found with the functions, emotions and innovation potential that lie beneath this mysterious and often inscrutable object. The purse is the ultimate repository for a woman, filled with beauty and disgust, function and emotion, pleasure, amusement, alarm and despair.

What inspired this work is hard to say, but most good ideas are a collision of things you've learned and things you're curious about. True insight is often revealed when you explore natural conflicts between what people believe or say or admit and what you observe in their habits, behavior and environment. This is the essence of observational research. I've been a market researcher, consumer strategist, and innovator for more than 20 years (yes, I was 12 when I started). I've observed consumers in stores, in homes, and even in the shower. I've watched people diaper their babies around the world and audited the contents of their medicine cabinets. In this work, I strive to reach higher and higher levels of insight to help my clients create innovations that will grow their businesses and products that consumers will love — love enough to part with their hard-earned cash in exchange for things that bring function and joy to life.

In the context of this work, I've seen literally hundreds, probably thousands, of women open their purses, both at home, where most consumer needs occur, and while shopping where most transactions are made and needs are fulfilled. Yet, they open this bag sparingly, revealing only what they must to get the job done. Like good burlesque, you see less than you think and you're left with your imagination to fill in the pasties.

There's probably something wrong with following a comment about stripping with a comment about your mom, but here goes. In terms of family taboos, nothing quite measured up to the sanctity of my mom's purse. We absolutely did not go in, or touch, or move this purse for any reason whatsoever. This, of course, shrouded it in delectable mystery.

Was it filled with gumdrops and kittens? Did it hold the mystery of the ages, revealed only to those worthy and willing to pay the price? Was it like Mary Poppins' bag of magical furniture and medicine? Was it where Nixon stashed the 18 minutes of missing tape? Who knew? What we knew was that nothing would bring such swift retribution as this particular form of trespass.

So, armed with curiosity and just enough knowledge to get into some real trouble, I set out to explore, reveal insights, and ultimately solve the mystery that is a women's purse. Each interview was voluntary, though respondents were paid for their time. Women were recruited between the ages of 18 and 64 in shopping malls in Portland, OR and Plano, TX — the "natural habitat" of the purse, so to speak. Respondents were recruited live and not allowed to make appointments. This kept them from editing the contents of their purses before the interview. I also did a concurrent telephone study to learn from a general sample the percentage of women who carry purses and the frequency of carrying them.

Each interview began with what I called "taking the baby to the pediatrician." The bag was weighed, measured and photographed. Each respondent was assigned a number to preserve anonymity. The photo of each bag with their number looked a lot like a mug shot. Next, respondents emptied all contents into a big pile. This looked exactly like a clown car at the circus. Visually, there was no way that the amount of stuff coming out could actually fit inside that space. It just kept coming and coming, item after item, and often didn't fit back in the bag when we were finished.

While emptying the bag, respondents were asked a series of questions regarding this specific purse: history, habits, likes/dislikes, and social status versus other purses in the household. The contents were sorted into groups according to whatever scheme was relevant to the respondent. Groups were named and inventoried, and photographs were taken of every object. Finally, a qualitative interview was conducted to reveal the bag's emotional role, context and the woman's history of carrying a purse. This quantitative and qualitative data was analyzed to reveal insight regarding the purse itself, each category of contents and what innovation opportunities exist within this home away from home. With women purchasing roughly 70% of all groceries and influencing most major purchases in the household, the role, influence and opportunity manifest in the purse cannot be underestimated.

Now, let me introduce you to 100 fascinating women and take you on a journey through uncharted territory — filled with danger and intrigue — the territory of the American Handbag.

Kelley Styring, Consumer Researcher

" The purse is the ultimate repository for a woman, filled with beauty and disgust, function and emotion, pleasure, amusement, alarm and despair.

...they open this bag sparingly, revealing only what they must to get the job done. Like good burlesque, you see less than you think and you're left with your imagination to fill in the pasties."

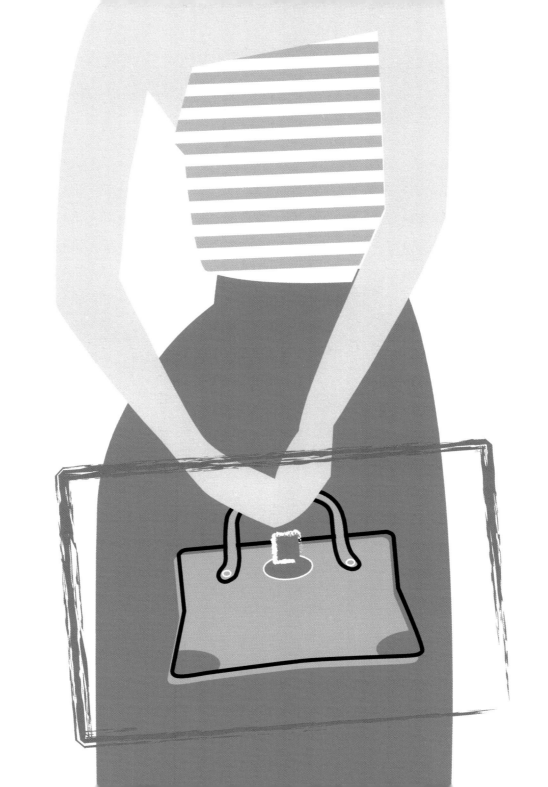

01.

Why did we do this study?

Most women who carry a purse cannot imagine how life would go on without it. They are passionate about the fact that it holds what they need to make it through the day. It is at once a financial center, a medicine cabinet, a pharmacy, a cosmetic counter, a communications hub, a safe-deposit box, and a stash for keepsakes of irreplaceable sentimental value. But, for every programmable PDA or cell phone there are a hundred little scraps of paper with important phone numbers scrawled on them. For every key, there is at least one key fob or doodad, not so much connecting the keys as marking the territory, making them easier to find and speaking out about the owner, her identity and where she's been in life.

The Purse is the only physical object that directly connects the home, where product needs are created, and the store, where those needs are fulfilled by transactions. With women purchasing roughly 70% of all groceries and influencing most major purchases in the household, the role, influence and opportunity manifest in the purse cannot be underestimated.

A woman's purse is a bag of contradiction on a string. It is the nerve center of her life — holding all manner of vital and precious things. Yet, most purses are a disorganized pit — mixing the tools of daily life — keys, wallet, phone, everything — with the detritus of living — gum wrappers, expired coupons, hair and general filth of every type. So, in short, the purse fails in its mission in terms of:

[organization • findability and durability of the items • hygiene and cleanliness • security]

Contradiction is where the genius of innovation lies. This study is a catalyst for innovation in an almost unlimited number of product categories. By studying the purse, the innovator can identify unmet and unarticulated needs by paying homage to the contradictions observed and build products to satisfy these

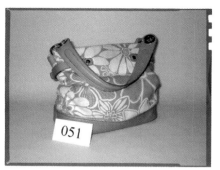

Each purse was weighed, measured, and photographed both as an object and carried by the owner. The purse was given a code name and number.

tropical blues – 051

needs. The first company to do that will win a spot in the purse and in the woman's heart as a consumer.

This study consists of 100 "Digs" including a qualitative and quantitative interview and inventory to delve into the context of the purse in a woman's life and the contents in detail, down to the last snotty tissue. A total of 100 women, 100 purses, 6670 items were examined and recorded down to the brand level. The objects weighed more than 300 pounds in total.

Each purse was weighed, measured, and photographed both as an object and as carried by the owner. The purse was given a code name and number (e.g. "TROPICAL BLUES" 051). This helped me personalize each woman and her purse, but maintain her anonymity. Questions delving into the history of the purse, the reasons for carrying it and its importance in her life were also explored.

Inventory information was coded and used to build a database for analysis. Qualitative interview information was analyzed for rich learning. And, the photographic evidence was examined to draw inferences and help better understand the quantitative and qualitative data.

The Big "So What?" – *Estimating the Innovation Opportunity*

There are almost 100 million women in the U.S. between the ages of 18 and 64. A full 95% of them carry a purse regularly, which means almost every single day. That's 88 million women to whom you can target innovation inspired by studying the purse. Given that each woman has 2.4 purses she uses regularly, you can actually increase the available sales potential to 212 million units if you plan to put your product in every single purse – which you should! Finally, for short purchase cycle products, or products that are purchased very frequently, the potential increases even further. For example, if your product is purchased once a month, that's 12 opportunities per year or 2.5 Billion units of opportunity you can access annually via this study.

the math

93,000,000 — { # of U.S. women aged 18-64

✗ 95% — { % who carry a purse "regularly"

88,000,000 → THIS IS THE NUMBER OF ADULT WOMEN WITH PURSES THAT FORM A TARGET GROUP FOR NEW PRODUCTS AND INNOVATIVE IDEAS THAT IMPROVE THE PURSE OR ITS CONTENTS.

✗ 2.4 — { # of purses carried "regularly"

212,000,000 → THIS IS THE NUMBER OF PURSES ACTIVELY CARRIED BY THOSE WOMEN. IF YOU PUT YOUR PRODUCT IN EVERY PURSE, THIS IS YOUR VOLUME POTENTIAL.

✗ 12 — { purchases per year for short purchase cycle categories

= 2,500,000,000

TOTAL PURCHASE OPPORTUNITIES

02.

First Purse Singular:
Why women begin carrying purses

My first purse was a beauty. Circa 1970, small gold metallic plastic with a cross-ball clasp and bright gold metal shoulder chain, this purse was second only in style to my Spider bike with the blue-green sparkly banana seat and "sissy" bar. When I carried this purse, I was sure my poop didn't stink. And, it was just big enough to hold a rather large rock I had planned to bring to school for show 'n' tell. I was in the second grade.

My teacher, Mrs. Eggloff, had to leave the room for some reason. At that age, you don't really think of teachers as using the bathroom, so I imagined her clutching coffee in the hall with the other teachers or just rambling around looking at things. Who knows? But, what I did know was that I was Class Monitor, which gave me absolute power for at least 5 minutes. I rose to take my position at the front of the class and gave them all my best steely stare. "Don't move" I said, through clenched teeth. It was at precisely this moment that this renegade kid, with his head clipper-clean for summer, leapt from his seat and began to run wildly through the rows, up and down, shouting, "You can't catch me! You can't catch me!"

I ran after him breathlessly for a few rows, then passed my own desk where my little gold bag dangled from the back of the chair. I snatched it cleanly without breaking stride and gave it a full hammer-throw over head twirl, bringing it down on the top of his head. *Crack* was the sound of my rock-filled purse on contact, a slight surprise to me since I'd forgotten entirely about the rock. He did stop running. He also started howling and bleeding a little, which was a bit of a problem for me as the teacher was just coming through the door. Both of us seized into stiff soldiers at the sight of her. I slunk back to my seat and he did the same, wiping his nose on his sleeve. No one ever spoke of the incident again, but my career as Class Monitor was officially over.

black tassel – 021   black studded – 050   large louis v – 028

There are two phases during which a woman first begins using a purse: 1) when she is young and uses it either for dress-up play or for special occasions like church or Easter Sunday, and 2) when she transitions from child to woman and has responsibility for her own stuff.

On the child side, many women relate a feeling of importance when they began carrying a purse in casual play or outings with the family. BLACK TASSEL 021 talked about seeing the "popular girls taking their purses with the long straps and swinging them around" with great envy. It was something she wanted to be a part of – a longing to be cool and grown-up. For others it was about emulating their mothers. BLACK STUDDED 050 started carrying a purse on a regular basis around age five. "I wanted to be just like Mommy. I carried it everywhere," she said.

For LARGE LOUIS-V 028 it was an important part of her Southern upbringing. "My mother gave it to me and said 'That's what girls carry.' She was Southern and very proper." 028 was four years old at the time. WOVEN AFFLUENCE 060's mother and grandmother bribed her into pulling her first tooth with the promise of a specific "Holly Hobby" purse she's been eyeing. It worked. She let them pull the tooth and got the purse. More than twenty years later, she beamed while telling this story. When MINI BACKPACK 032 was about ten years old her mother said "You're becoming a young lady and you need to carry things." She bought her daughter her first purse. Her daughter filled it with dolls.

Early to mid-teens is another important entry point for carrying a purse. Women begin to menstruate and need the security and privacy a purse provides to carry their supplies. Teenaged women also have grown-up responsibilities, like driving and holding down a job. Both of these things require tools like Identification, Driver's Licenses, Keys and Cash that are typically carried in a purse. TROPICAL BLUES 051 said "I used to put stuff in my pockets. But, stuff falls out of your pockets. I lost a debit card that

woven affluence – 060

mini backpack – 032

don't wanna be here – 072

way. Then, I started carrying a purse." The purse is a gateway for girls to the responsibilities of a woman — and an entry point for marketers to reach an important young audience.

The opportunity to carry a secret stash of things has strong allure for teens. DON'T WANNA BE HERE 072 was enamored with her first purse. "People thought I had something important in there," she said. And, she was right. Purses carry all manner of important things that teen aged women want to hide, particularly from their mothers. Cigarettes, makeup, pictures of boys, birth control, and even drugs are common items sheltered in the sanctity of the young woman's purse. Like BABY GIRL 017 put it, "You can't just walk around with tampons and drugs in your hands." Some women also respond to the insecurity they feel as they spend more time in a hostile adult world by carrying weapons such as knives and pepper spray. We found no guns in this study, but we're sure they're out there.

"Purses carry all manner of important things that teen aged women want to hide...Cigarettes, make-up, pictures of boys, birth control, and even drugs are common items sheltered in the sanctity of the young woman's purse."

"I had my daughter and woke up to needing emergency things"

barely there – 063

As a young woman becomes an adult, her responsibilities grow. She'll start carrying a planner and other devices to organize her time. She'll transition fully from a backpack or school bag that may have been doubling as a purse into a traditional handbag. New moms talk about the increasing importance of the purse when their child was born. "I had my daughter and woke up to needing emergency things," related BARELY THERE 063.

And PUBLIC TRANSPORTATION 069 said, "When my first child was a baby, I carried a diaper bag. As she grew up, it evolved into more of a purse."

We can see a clear pattern in terms of the size and weight of purses related to age of the woman. The younger women carry compact, precise purses with fewer items. Moms and women who feel responsible for other people carry bigger and more complexly loaded bags. Older women, late Baby Boomers, carry small purses, a bit more complex in their contents than a young woman's, but definitely a compact carry compared to the middle group.

I see this same pattern in myself. I carried small, stylish bags when I was a teen and young adult, and a large, hulking diaper bag then traditional large purse when my kids were babies and toddlers. Now that they're pre-teens, I'm down to a wallet on a string, with nothing but cash, ID and a cell phone holster. I think I went extreme in my transition because I got tired of carrying everyone else's stuff. And, I decided that if I didn't provide the things everyone needs in the blink of an eye that they might grow more self sufficient or learn to do without. Neither of these is a bad thing to know how to do. So, my purse is now less of a Department Store and more of a six-gun in a shoulder holster, ready for a shootout, but not prepared to stitch up a wound, treat a snakebite, or host a potluck dinner. And, I'm okay with that.

public transportation - 069

"When my first
child was a baby,
I carried a diaper
bag. As she grew
up, it evolved into
more of a purse."

03.

Feminism and Femininity:
The purse as a link to womanhood

The purse is a font of femininity — not just in an obvious way, as a holder of tampons, but also as an accessory expressing personality of the owner. Some women are strictly rational, selecting a bag that's the right size or maybe matches their shoes or outfit. Others are emotional about the functionality — specialized pockets, built-in wallets, umbilicals to attach change purses and makeup bags inside really push their buttons. Still others are emotional about the bag's appearance and what a "cute" bag says about them as women. In any case, the purse is a symbol of womanhood and, in the eyes of merchants, the woman's historical rise as a visible consumer or purchasers of goods for the household.

The purse is a symbol of transition from girl to woman. Whether this transition is prompted by menstruation and the need to conceal the pads and tampons associated with that or whether it is prompted by the desire to be more "grown-up" carrying a purse on a day-to-day basis is associated with womanhood. Soon, as responsibility builds, a young woman learns to drive or gets her first job, and the role of the purse expands. It becomes the safe storage and transport device for money, identification and keys. She becomes more responsible for herself and the purse is a vital supporting tool. When she is mature, paths of emotional depth develop that go beyond wanting to feel like a woman and being responsible for the basics. What emerges is a strong, almost compulsive need to be prepared for any situation that might occur. The stronger this need, the more items and categories represented in the bag. Specifically, two links to emotional health are evident:

1) a basic need for security rooted in preparedness for any situation that affects them, their loved ones, and even the public at large including strangers — this is rooted in the fear of failure, and

"a woman with a purse didn't need a man with pockets to make her way through the world and she became a consumer in the eyes of the marketplace"

2)   the empowerment achieved by being prepared for any situation and the reflection of this preparedness on them as a successful woman or mom. This is rooted in the esteem achieved.

Always having an adhesive bandage at the ready is the modern female equivalent of the six-gun of the Wild West. My father no sooner nicked his finger on a drill bit at the hardware store than a woman reached with pointed directness for a secret stash in her purse producing not only a bandage to stem the flow of the offending blood but antibiotic ointment just in case he was in danger of infection. Similar scenes play themselves out everyday as women feel good about themselves for being prepared. And, why shouldn't they? Making your way through each day feeling successful can add up to a successful feeling in life in general, even if you do derive your satisfaction from an adhesive bandage.

Beyond femininity and self-esteem, the purse is also a periodic repository for the tools of sexual freedom. Storing condoms, lubricants, birth control pills and even receipts for porn is not only common, but it also accommodates a spontaneous life. If the woman doesn't know where she'll be on any given night, but she knows wherever she is she'll be proximal to her purse, where else would she keep what she needs? This is particularly true for younger age groups because the needs for these items are more prevalent, and let's face it, the opportunity occurs more often.

The independence manifest in the handbag is potentially related to its history, though I'm piecing this together a bit here. First, we know from early documents and engravings that people carried drawstring pouches, typically at the waist, in which they placed their money, valuables and even flint to create fire on the spot. Talk about needing to be prepared. This pouch may have evolved from an early seed bag used in the fields by peasants. We know that at some point men's trousers developed pockets, or an

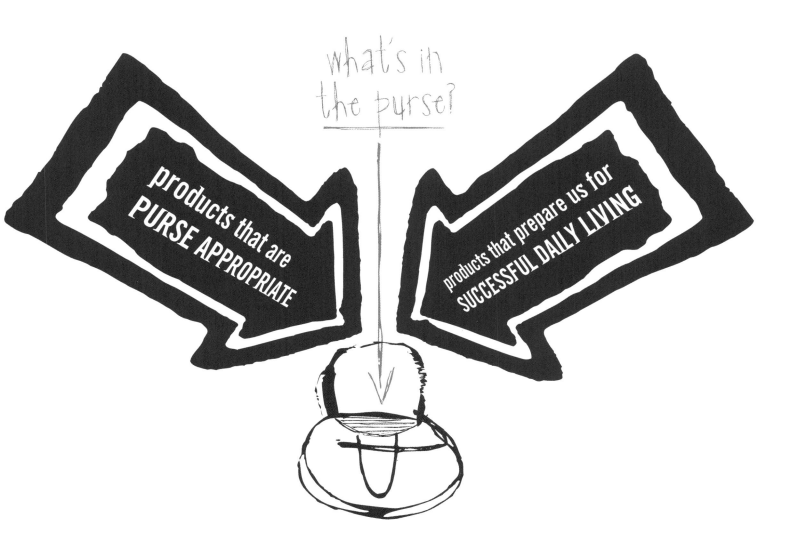

what's in the purse?

products that are **PURSE APPROPRIATE**

products that prepare us for **SUCCESSFUL DAILY LIVING**

inside purse so to speak and women carried their pouch in the layers of their skirts. As fashion styles moved away from abundant layers, a woman's purse became visible. Purses then became symbols of style, but probably more importantly symbols of independence. A woman with a purse didn't need a man with pockets to make her way through the world, and she became a consumer in the eyes of the marketplace.

04.

Husbands, Lovers and Lounge Lizards:
Emotions that drive purse and content choice

Most of the time, there is no particular need driving the purchase of a new purse. A woman might be browsing through a store or mall, looking for other things or nothing in particular at all. Like an attractive man in a crowded bar, the purse catches her eye. She considers whether he's an upgrade to her current lover or whether he's a good fit for her stable of choices, depending on her particular lifestyle — or purse-style that is. If it's on sale, that's often the clincher to at least have a one-nighter and see how it goes. It's not every purse you can live with long term, but there are plenty that make for a swell afternoon.

The selection of a particular purse is an odd cocktail of rational and emotional needs, all readily expressed without reservation. "It keeps me organized" is heard just as often as "It was cute" which doesn't happen very often with consumer products. Typically, with other types of products, one strain or the other will supersede, with the rational choice often taking the front seat, assigning the emotional desire to the baby seat in the back. The rational might be used to justify an emotional purchase, but it's not typically up front and personal. The selection and adoption of a purse works differently.

GANG OF FOUR: A RATIONAL AND EMOTIONAL MATRIX

There are four constructs expressed that describe the relationship a woman has with her purse and how this relationship affects both her purchase of purses and uses of those she currently owns:

1) a bag I put my crap in
2) basically organized and sized to do the job
3) cleverly organized, and
4) cute as hell

a rational / emotional matrix

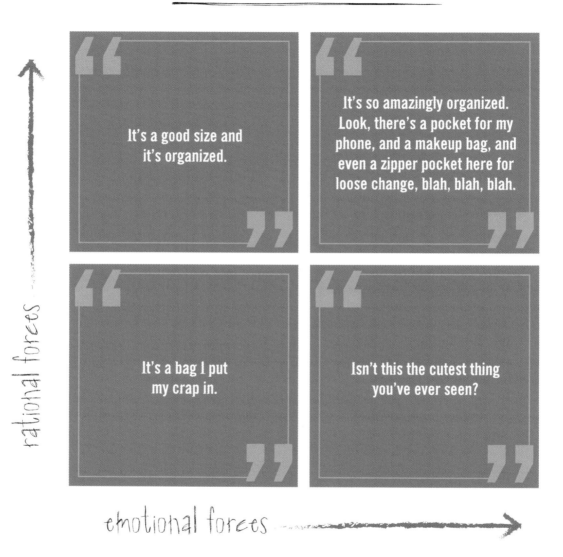

rational forces

emotional forces

" It's a good size and it's organized. "

" It's so amazingly organized. Look, there's a pocket for my phone, and a makeup bag, and even a zipper pocket here for loose change, blah, blah, blah. "

" It's a bag I put my crap in. "

" Isn't this the cutest thing you've ever seen? "

Each of these designations blends a particular level of rational thought and emotional reaction to the bag.

Many, many women say their purse is a bag they put their "crap" in. When asked why it's important to have a purse, they can't get much farther than that. When asked what they would do if purses didn't exist, they say they'd reach for a plastic grocery sack or even carry fewer things so they'd fit in their pockets. There's not a shred of emotion at work here, and very little rational logic either. In the two-by-two matrix, this is the lower left block — not particularly emotional or rational about this thing. It's just something they use and any substitute would work for them.

Another group of women say their purse has basic functions in life and is sized correctly to do the job. They believe it does have a role in their life, to keep things organized and at hand, but they're not particularly passionate about it. As BABY GIRL 017 put it "You can't carry your drugs and tampons around in your hand." These women fall in the upper left quadrant of the matrix — highly rational, but not very emotional about their purses.

A third group of women say that their purses improve their ability to function in the world. Often their purses are cleverly organized, filled with many specialized compartments and features like built-in wallets, cell phone holsters, etc. Frequently, these purses are purchased as part of a mission to become more organized or replace a beloved purse that filled this function. But, while rational in motivation, these women readily give emotional responses when asked about the importance of their purse. It's a rational construct, emotionally expressed: "I'd be lost without it" or "It's my life" are common responses. They literally can't imagine functioning in a world without purses and get a stricken look on their faces when asked this particular question. This group falls in the upper right quadrant of the matrix — highly rational, but with a highly emotional rationale.

"laddering" exercise example

Researcher: "How important is your purse to you?"

Respondent: "Very" ←——— (almost 100% of our sample gave this specific response)

Researcher: "In what way is it very important to have a purse?"

Respondent: "It carries everything I need."

Researcher: "Why is it important to carry everything you need?"

(respondent thinks: "that's a dumb question.")

Respondent: "So I can be prepared for what might happen during my day."

Researcher: "Why is important to be prepared for what might happen during your day?"

(respondent thinks: "i've never met someone so stupid")

Respondent: "Because I never know what I'm going to need."

Researcher: "Why is it important to you to have what you're going to need?"

The final group is a group just having fun. Yes, the bag holds their things, but isn't it the cutest thing you ever saw? They tend to have a variety of purses at home and change the bag to fit their outfit or mood, though some are deeply in love with a single bag and have a more monogamous relationship with it. These bags tend to be brighter in color and ornamented. They don't tend to have a specialized function. Sure, everything might not fit in this bag, but isn't it cute? "I just had to have it" is the most common reason for purchase and these purchases are almost always spontaneous. This group falls into the lower right block of the matrix: highly emotional, not very rational. But, aren't they cute?

PYRAMID OF PURSES: AN EMOTIONAL HIERARCHY

In 1943, Abraham Maslow published his paper called "A Theory of Human Motivation." This simple, yet elegant premise is that as basic needs are satisfied, more sophisticated and emotional needs manifest, thus motivating a human being through life and to higher levels of achievement and satisfaction. This research on handbags uses a process related to Maslow's work called "laddering." With this technique, the interviewer asks about the purse and what it does for the woman in daily life. The question sequence then asks 'why' each response is important using the woman's own words in a reflective style. For the

(respondent thinks: "how can i get a job like this so i can be paid to be so stupid?")

Respondent: "So that I can function. I don't want to be caught without what I need."

Researcher: "How does it make you feel when you don't get caught without what you need?"

(respondent thinks: "oh, this is weird")

Respondent: "Secure." "Comfortable that I can handle things."

Researcher: "How does it make you feel about yourself that you can handle things?"

(respondent thinks: "am i in therapy?")

Respondent: "Like a capable person." "Like a good mom."

Researcher: "Why is it important to be seen as a capable person?"

(respondent thinks: "give me my thirty bucks, i'm outta here")

Respondent: "It makes me feel good about myself, like I can do anything."

respondent, it's a little like talking to a two-year-old child. For the researcher, it requires you to behave like you're dumb as a bucket of rocks. But, the results are revealing and consistent across the 100 interviews.

In this laddering chain, we move slowly from the purse as an object to carry things around into its deeper role as an instrument of capability. Self-esteem is related strongly to capability. You can tell your children how great they are and it will make them feel happy to a certain extent. But, give them capability and the opportunity to demonstrate that they are capable and their self-esteem will soar off the chart. This is the true role of the purse for most women. All respondents in this study make it to the "security" level of this hierarchy, but about half can go all the way to self-esteem and achievement in the world. This is impressive given that they don't give this type of thought to their purses, ever.

Those who fall into the emotional or "isn't it cute?" quadrant of the matrix demonstrate just as much ability to ladder up to self-esteem and achievement as those who are on the hyper-organized or rational sides of the model. That's because, no matter what the path toward attachment, the attachment between woman and purse is very, very strong and rooted in emotional needs.

pyramid of purses: an emotional hierarchy

aspirational needs   "I am the best woman/ mom that i can be."

esteem needs   "I am efficient and capable."

social needs   "I feel like I can handle anything."

safety needs   "So I feel prepared."

hygiene needs   "It carries everything I need."

maslow's hierarchy

THE CIRCLE OF PREPAREDNESS

Preparedness is a function that women assume in life and it's related strongly to their role as caregivers for family, friends, and even total strangers. Within the bag, its contents are weighted according to what I'll call their "Circle of Preparedness." At the center of the circle is the woman herself. The objects in the purse that are at the epicenter of the Circle of Preparedness are those she needs to leave the house and enter the world: Wallet, Keys, Identification, and Communication Devices. The second ring of the circle includes immediate family — husband, lover, and/or kids. The woman perceives herself as a vital cog in the machinery of family life and her purse is the toolbox when they're out of the home. During any scourge that happens, she wants to make sure she has the right weapon to fight it: hair bands, adhesive bandages, sewing kits, toilet seat covers, you name it. The arsenal is deep. The woman feels gratified when she can whip out the right tool for the job without hesitation. All she needs is "thanks" to light up with satisfaction. She feels capable.

The outer ring of the Circle of Preparedness includes acquaintances and even strangers. While waiting for a plane in a busy airport, I was seated near a toddler with nothing to do. Now, toddlers create their own fun in busy airports with nothing to do and this is never a good thing for their parents or anyone within earshot. With the speed of a superhero ducking into a phone booth, I whipped open my bag, shot my hand to the bottom and without hesitation brought out a fast food kids-meal toy. I knew it was there. I just didn't know when I would need it. And, here I was — hero in a moment. Crisis averted, I saw a nail file too, which kept me busy, which is a good thing because delayed in a crowded airport, I can become a toddler pretty quickly. That's how the outer ring of the circle works. You are prepared for other people's crises and act without hesitation. This combination of preparedness and selfless sacrifice endears you to others publicly and feels good.

The need to be prepared and its consequences drive the categories included in the purse from financial services and cosmetics, to first-aid and entertainment items. Understanding the need to be prepared and discovering the link between the product categories is one route to innovation. There are countless other categories that are not highly represented in the collective purse, that are vital to preparedness: like food and beverage. Successful innovators will develop products that meet this need for preparedness but are also purse appropriate. Products that satisfy needs for esteem by enabling women to be more capable in their mobile and busy environment will win a spot in the purse and win competitively in the marketplace.

Insight: "Innovators will recognize the importance of the need to be prepared and its link to self-esteem. Products that satisfy needs for esteem by enabling women to be more capable in their mobile, busy life will win a spot in the purse and win competitively in the marketplace."

05.

Dog Days:
The life cycle of the purse

I am sitting on a plane in Dallas, TX and wondering hard about how I got into this mess. It's 109 degrees outside and feels like 102 inside this plane. I swear you could roast your own peanuts. We take off and the combination of fresh air and meal service makes me feel a little bit queasy. I start to pick at my food, a weird combination of pesto, obscure creamy-based sauce and circus striped tortellini, flaccid on the inside and just crispy enough on the edges to remind you of a six-pack carton that's been wet and then dried in the sun beside a dumpster. Point of fact, this meal looks exactly like it was scraped from a garbage can -- except for the fact that I'm in first class, both a little drunk and lot hungry, and not eating snack mix in steerage. It's just about the most delicious meal I've ever seen. You see, it's all about context.

And, that's how I got into this mess. I'm in the second week of interviewing women about their purses, interviews 46 – 90 in fact, and Dallas is the perfect town for this*. In Dallas, they purse like nobody's business. And, Plano is the "Dallas" of Dallas, so that's where I went, Plano TX, population 250,000 plus and at least one million purses full of net worth. Plano is a spending town. I read once that people don't move to Texas for the purple mountain's majesty. And, they don't move there for the waving fields of grain. They move to there to make money. And, make it they do. It's a very successful town full of successful people. Mile upon mile of McMansions smear across the landscape as far as your eye can see, punctuated by the occasional or more than occasional mall and BMW dealership. This town knows how to live and how to spend. All of this requires a purse and usually a person operating that purse who is experienced with spending.

* the balance of the interviews were conducted in portland, or a town equally unique but not detailed in this report

Again, it's all about context. When you live in an upscale, competitive place like Plano, TX (which I did for six years), you become part of the culture of consumption. This is an important point, because consumer trends are discovered, set and fulfilled by people who live and grow and raise kids and run businesses in places like Plano, TX. It's a cycle and places like Plano are the fuel of consumption. And, into that cycle we all go, because as goes Plano, goes the Nation. Scary, but true.

So, we go to Plano and dig. We ask questions. We drink coffee, lots of coffee. And, we learn some things – like, when you direct interest toward a woman's purse, she'll say it's the most important thing in her life. It fills her daily destiny. It is lover, friend, matriarch and dominatrix. It is dependent and enabling. It's frigging co-dependent. Yet, in the totality of her life, it's not the most important thing. In fact, it's not even fifth.

We didn't ask this question, but I'm gonna go with God, country, family, pets, fame, fortune, etc. as the list of priorities that probably edge out the purse and there are likely a hundred more. So, while it's her number-one organizational tool, it's still an afterthought in the big scheme of life.

Now, by coincidence, when I'm in Dallas, I'm not only conducting these interviews but also studying the health habits of Americans for a beverage company and writing new product concepts for dogs. Well, not concepts FOR dogs, or for TYPES of dogs, but for dog food for dogs and for types of dogs. Though, as innovations go, a written language for dogs to read themselves would be right up there with ketchup. My mind starts rambling through all these corridors at once and I start to wonder if a dog is a good metaphor for the life stages of a purse.

First, you have the puppy stage -- developmentally important and filled with infatuation. This new bag may be a keeper or it may not. It may absorb all of your life's necessities black-hole-like, or it may not. If not, will you get rid of the puppy or the torn up couch? Who knows? You have to work up to that algebra on your own, but secretly, you know it has a lot to do with how cute that "puppy purse" is. Think of all the crap you've taken and bad movies you've watched just to gaze on beautiful people. You'll put up with a lot for beauty and you know it.

Then, you have the adult "dog purse" stage and you are in love. You and your "dog purse" are in a groove. Inseparable, you operate in a fully non-verbal mode. Needs are accommodated and healthy habits maintained. Neither of you may get a bath as often as you would like, but the basics are there. Things function and they fit in a very real way.

The "senior purse" stage is the tough stage. If you have forgotten about the "puppy purse" stage and there is no obvious damage to table legs or base boards to remind you, this Senior stage is a relentless bag of deteriorating function and increasing emotional attachment. And, somehow there's always pee on the carpet. Finally, the zipper breaks, the strap comes loose or the bowels are unmanageable and the "purse dog" has to go to a happier place. And, unless you spring for cremation, they both end up

black beaded – 044

at the dump.

The biggest difference is that a lifelong companion, like a beloved dog, gives more to you in a glance than you do to it with a lifetime of care and affection. You don't run right out and replace it like you do your purse. And, there's no stash of former favorites or wedding special discard dogs in the closet to tide you over. And, as BLACK BEADED 044 might agree - you can't replace your dog with a Zip-loc bag. Well . . . not unless you're very, very well medicated.

06.

Postcards from the Purse:
Stories that reveal emotional connection

My grandfather was a collector. He collected washing machines, slum homes, and friends by the dozen. When he passed away, I was about twenty and disposing of the treasures of his life was an all-family effort and endlessly fascinating. His stuff was cool. I was in his bedroom going through some clothes when I crouched down, gently lifting the bedcovers where they draped to the floor and peering into the darkness under the bed. As my eyes adjusted, I could see the reflection of two reptilian eyes looking my general direction from about four feet away. I can't even describe the sound I made as I shrieked my way across the floor and back against the nearest wall. Did I mention that we were in Florida? And, what I saw was a 'gator, at least 3 feet long, but growing larger in my mind with every breath. Nothing moved.

No one came to help me either, which was slightly annoying. I waited for what felt like two hours but was probably closer to ten minutes. There was a broom on the floor. With one hand, I reached for the broom and used it to lift the bedcovers and peek under the bed once more. At this point, I discovered a lovely alligator skin handbag in perfect condition, still bearing the head and feet of the original owner. The blank prosthetic eyes stared at me and a promise was made. "You are mine -- forever." I carried that bag every day for two years, enduring the shock of strangers and derision of those who objected to the ornamental use of endangered species. It was the perfect accessory in the 80s era of punk rock and worse. It hangs on my wall today. I'll always wonder where my grandfather got such a thing and what it was doing under his bed. I hope the owner was as wild as he was. There wasn't a thing in it to help me understand. But, it doesn't matter. It's mine, as is the moment I found it.

Some years earlier I was spending a week with my grandmother. I was about ten years old. We liked to eat sunflower seeds and drink beer (I got a shot-glass-sized portion) while watching the soaps, which she called her "stories." This particular summer, she'd acquired a new kitten. Cats did sort of seem to come and go around her, but this one was a sweet red tabby that she adored and was a highlight of my summer visit.

My grandmother decided that she needed to go to the Kash 'n Karry to get some Puss 'n Boots canned cat food for the little kitty. I loved this brand because it had the little character on it and her loyalty to this brand was absolute even though it smelled exactly like the bottom of a garbage can. But, she didn't want to leave the kitty alone in the house while we went to the grocery. So, she grabbed her woven rattan bag with the big blue-and-green flowers on it, and without a moment's hesitation stuffed both her smokes and the kitty in her purse, zipped it up, and climbed into the big old Chevy Bel Air for the ride to the store. She mashed on the gas and let in a blessed plume of fresh air — a good thing since the car was not air conditioned, it was Florida in the summer, and she smoked. The kitty in the bag was fairly subdued, likely due to lack of oxygen and oppressive heat.

"Each story is a memory that illuminates the emotional connection of a woman to her purse in a particular moment."

After about ten minutes in the store he began to revive, however, and the bag began to take on a life of its own. Loud, long, low growling howls of "let me the hell out of here" began to emanate from my grandmother's shoulder, attracting cautious glances and some outright stares. She just continued to shop and smoke and ignore the whole thing unfolding under her very own arm, looking around every once in a while as if the sound could be coming from somewhere else, until we left the store and freed the freaked-out kitty in the car. This bought us a ride home with the windows almost all the way up, where we both could have had a heat stroke, but the kitty was free and safe to freak out all over the inside of the car. Beer and soaps was sounding pretty good about this time.

These stories while true and colorful aren't very unusual when you ask a woman for a story about her purse or purses of the past. Each story is a memory that illuminates the emotional connection of a woman to her purse in a particular moment. The better we understand these moments, the more effectively we can market innovations that improve the purse, the contents and her relationship to them.

LAS VEGAS 056 purchased her beautiful casino themed bag with her winnings at the blackjack table. She told a fantastic story about how she and her sister, when they were young, hid the box of oatmeal in the cedar chest which also held their Easter dresses. They did this because they hated oatmeal and thought, correctly, that if their mother couldn't find it, she couldn't make them eat it. Weeks later, Easter Sunday services were disrupted as a field mouse, probably after oatmeal in the cedar chest, popped out of her Easter purse while she was sitting in the front pew directly across from the choir. The

las vegas — 056

orst at 44 – 070

little black bag – 011

sister golden hair – 089

minister never missed a beat, but the choir was caught laughing as the little mouse skittered away in front of the pulpit.

Several women related stories of being cajoled or pressured into getting a purse for the first time. A few mothers and grandmothers took them shopping for purses so they would be a "young lady" and "carry important things, like Barbie dolls." Many trips for a first purse also included a first lipstick. FIRST AT 44 070 was married for the first time at age 44. Her new husband bought her a purse so that she would be more 'ladylike.' Prior to this time, she carried everything she needed in a small Zip-loc bag in her pocket.

Quite a few women have left a purse behind on a bus or in church, and while they're frequently recovered, the women are definitely left reeling from the lost feeling of being without their bag. When a purse is stolen and not recovered, the loss is felt in three ways:

1) the risk of identity theft and actual theft via loss of financial documents, credit cards, etc.,
2) the emotional loss of photographs and keepsakes that are irreplaceable, and
3) losing a purse tended to shake their sense of security.

The emotional loss is a harder blow from which they often don't recover fully. This is manifest in high protectiveness of their current bag or stripping of the bag of all sentimentality — bringing only what they absolutely need to make it through the day.

LITTLE BLACK BAG 011 mentioned that her mother said a purse was a safe place to put things like a knife or pepper spray. We found several weapons ranging from mace to switchblades and even one case where the purse itself was used for protection. PUBLIC TRANSPORTATION 069 was riding a bus home from work when she was accosted by a man who appeared to be very drunk. She moved behind the driver and told

big buckle – 080

pony express – 082

seat covers – 086

him to leave her alone. When he persisted and the driver was no help, she hit him with her purse until the bus driver stopped and threw her off the bus. The purse became a weapon, and an effective one at that.

Several women, including SISTER GOLDEN HAIR 089, left their purse on the roofs of their cars and drove off. In some cases the purse was rescued when neighbors or passers by gesticulated wildly to call attention to the situation. "Sister Golden Hair" 089 had no such luck as she arrived at her destination without her purse. Going back home for it, she found the contents crushed to a pulp in the parking lot of her apartment complex. Funny thing is, she's pretty sure she ran over it herself as she remembered running over something in the parking lot that morning.

Some of the stories regarding purses occurred very early in life and are filled with the warmth of distant memory. BIG BUCKLE 080 carried her mother's big purse around the house, day after day, for dress-up until she fell and knocked out a tooth. She also used her own first purse to hit a Sunday school teacher who mispronounced her name. Other memories are painful, such as PONY EXPRESS 082 who carried a small change purse given to her by her parents until she lost it. They were disappointed and she still feels the hurt of that loss as an adult.

Many women carry so many things in their purse that they lose track of precisely what's in there. SEAT COVERS 086 carries such an array of items that she keeps a second purse in her trunk for extra things she might need "just in case." This collection and its relative disarray in the bag has also created a situation where items are lost in the very environment deemed most safe, available, and convenient in which to store them. HIP REPLACEMENT 078 stated she frequently loses things that later turned up in her purse, making the purse itself at once a treasure chest, black hole, and host of surprise.

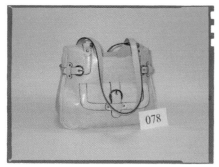

hip replacement – 078

"The purse is not only a functional item and source of emotional comfort and control. It is a symbol of womanhood and, as such, has a unique link to each woman's history.
In some cases memories of purses are fun and charming, in other cases these memories represent loss and the tinge of sadness that's a part of growing up. In all cases, these memories are part of the very substance of the woman who carries the purse and the purse is a conduit to her world."

07.

Killing You Softly:
Why your purse is hazardous to your health

I have a friend who calls his wife's purse the "B-BOD." This is short for 'black bag of death." I've never personally examined this particular specimen, but he suggests it weighs more than their newborn daughter. And, he's probably right. In fact, it's so heavy that he can't stand to see her struggle to carry it and often offers to carry it for her.

While the purses in this study range in weight from a little less than a pound to more than six pounds, the median (most common) weight is 3.6 lbs. That means that more than half of the women in our study carry more than three and a half pounds on their shoulder every single day. That doesn't sound like much, but putting that much strain on the neck and shoulders definitely takes a toll. There have been many articles written in the popular press on this topic and our research confirms their suspicions. Purses are heavy and put weight on one side of the body, resulting in soreness, stiff necks and sometimes even back and hip pain.

Apparently purses carry not only important items for daily living — but more germs than a Petri dish. According to recent news reports, the exterior of a purse can host pseudomonas (that cause eye infection), staphylococcus aureus (that cause skin infection), and even E-coli and salmonella (that cause intestinal infection). It seems these germs are picked up by putting the purse on the floor, particularly in places like public restrooms, and putting the purse on your countertop or table at home is bringing those germs right back where you live. In fact, it's said that if you put your purse on the kitchen counter, you may as well take your shoes off and put them right next to it. It's just that gross.

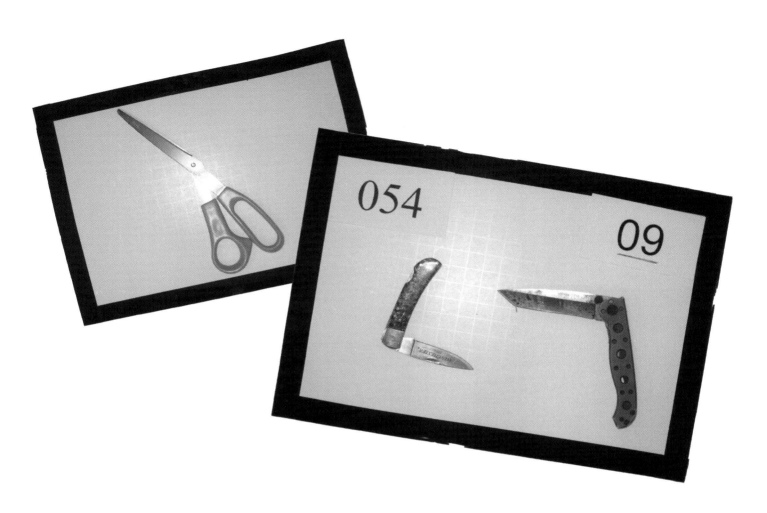

Women carry sharp objects in their purses and often jam their hands inside to "look" for things by sense of touch because they can't see inside. It's dark and deep. About 14% of all women carry some sort of knife. Six percent carry scissors. And, 80% carry pens/pencils, all of which can hurt you if you're not looking.

There were moments during this study when I wondered if I was in danger. I was talking with women while handling their concealed weapons. I was talking to women and identifying their tuberculosis meds. Was she contagious? I was handling mysterious bottles with unidentifiable chemical contents. Were they drugs? Was this person high? Some of these purses contained indescribable odors and filth. Purse are rarely cleaned and contain the debris of everyday life, so yeah, they smell. In fact, I went through two big tubs of antibacterial wipes used to clean the tables and my hands between each interview.

So, to protect yourself from <u>your own</u> purse:

> watch the weight

> clean it out every so often and lighten the load

> look inside before jamming your hand in there

this advice can be extrapolated to your entire life.

> wipe the outside with soapy water or an antibacterial wipe

> try not to put it on the floor

there are also superstitions that suggest you'll lose your entire fortune if you put your purse on the floor, so more than one good reason not to put it there.

> try not to put it on the countertop, table, or other food handling area

To protect yourself from <u>other people's</u> purses:

> don't rummage around in anyone else's purse, you don't know what's in there!

> be nice, a woman with a purse could be armed!

> wash your hands often → your mom told you to do this, and i'm saying it again. you'll get sick less and you'll thank us both

014

011

019

052

the purses

018

062

013

036

08.

Meet the Purses

Like kids on Halloween, purses come in an almost unimaginable range of styles, sizes and configurations. In fact, some were just as scary. In this study, there were 8 basic purse types observed, the most common of which is the Sausage, so named because it is longer than it is wide. The Sausage Style is well-liked because it has a wide mouth and light can penetrate its shallow body, allowing women to see the contents even if the bag is quite large. A full 20% of women in this study carry a Sausage Style purse and they hold 88 items on average.

The second most popular style is actually a tie. The Micro Bag is prized for its size, or lack thereof. It's a "go anywhere" choice with little room for overload. It's carried by 18% of women and holds 39 items on average. Tied with the Micro at 18% is the External Pocket Purse — named for the many pouches and pockets slapped on the outside for maximum organization. Holding 78 items on average, this is the shoulder holster of purses -- with items stored for fast access like a six-gun in the Old West.

The fourth most popular style is the Slouch, so called for its lack of structure. When placed on a table, it flops over like a big lazy dog. This purse is a close cousin to the Tote in its catch-all attitude and bad posture. Soft and cozy, this bag is enjoyed for its friendly textures and suppleness. It holds 56 items on average and is carried by 14% of all women.

The Tote also holds 56 items on average and women rummage through this style of purse to exhaustion. Carried by 13% of all women, the Tote is a catch-all, containing all the typical, expected items along with many forgotten, unexpected things.

It's all about style with the Bling group, carried by 9% of all women and carrying 85 items on average. This bag is bold and sassy and not just for a big night out on the town. Paired as often with blue jeans at the mall as a nice pair of heels, this bag has no organizational intent – it's showy and fun all the way.

The Upscale Print purse is carried by 5% of women and holds 83 items on average. For this bag style, it's all about the print and the print is all about the brand and badging yourself with the brand is more important than the bag's size or function. Branding the carrier of the bag is its most important job, though carriers of this group of bags deny it!

Finally, the Mini Backpack was the least frequently observed style of purse in this study. Only 3% of women carry this bag, which acts much like a Tote, but distributes the weight across two shoulders. It holds 43 items on average.

One purse in this study was as heavy as a healthy newborn, weighing in at more than six pounds, but the purses weighed 3.4 lbs on average including all contents. The average measurement is 11 inches in length, 5 and a half inches in width and nearly 8 inches in height. The total cubic inches of space in the average handbag is nearly 500 inches. That's a lot of storage space, particularly for something carried in one hand and on one shoulder by 95% of women. In fact, this figure is like a light switch – it's on or it's off. Women carry a purse at least once a week with 75% of women carry one every day. Only 5% never carry a purse. There is no in between.

One woman in this study claimed to have 115 purses in her collection, but most women own just over 10 purses. On a regular basis, they use 2 to 3 different purses, with one in four changing daily or weekly. The majority of purses are purchased during the late spring and early summer, in May, June and July.

There is another small seasonal bump in purchases in late fall stretching through holiday months, but it is a fraction of the rise in purchases in the warmer weather time period. Most purses observed in this research were relatively new, purchased either that year or the year before. Only about a third of the purses were more than two years old.

Half of all purses are purchased at Department Stores and Mass Merchandisers. The balance are scattered across specialty boutiques, shoe stores, etc. This helps explain the very high propensity toward "unbranded" purses or small, unknown brands (80% of all purses). Black is the most common purse color, followed by brown and beige. However, 45% of all purses carried are brightly colored, patterned and festooned with decoration. The high variety of design styles makes it difficult to aggregate them by specific color, but when considered as "colorful" they far outnumber the bland black, brown and beige.

Like a good friend, a woman's purse is generally well-liked, with more than 80% of women claiming to like their purse "extremely or very well." That said, when they describe what they like, it's all about the styling. "It's so cute." "It matches my outfit." But, when asked why they're carrying the particular purse they're carrying on the day of the interview, the responses are rational and tend toward functional and ergonomic issues. "It has lots of pockets." "It holds everything I need." This dichotomy between the emotional "likes" and the rational "reasons why carry" reveal significant insight regarding the purse itself and what drives purchase and usage. This is underscored by the reasons women dislike their purses. They cite age and worn appearance, as well as size (too small) and ergonomics. This suggests that while style may drive purchase, function drives usage, and the innovator who solves for both would have the recipe for category loyalty when it comes time to replace a purse.

(see emotional vs. rational matrix, p30)

phones religious items security&access

beauty jewelry cameras feminine

healthcare identification remotes

oral care keepsakes candy

finance coupons

gun security

hair care

nail care photographs weapons

office supplies trash food

tissues

09.

What's in the purse?

More than 30 product categories are represented in the purse, truly making it a home away from home. There are 15 product categories that are contained in more than half of all purses — demonstrating the vital nature of these items that they must be carried on her person everyday.

Access to finances comprises the most important category of items in the purse, including wallet, checkbook, credit cards, cash and bank cards. Cell Phones and Keys comprise the rest of the top tier of items. Second tier items include Medications, Sunglasses and Beauty Care items. Third tier items include Cigarettes, Glasses and Schedulers/Planners. If you've ever asked a woman to carry something for you in her purse — DON'T! When asked to rank the importance of other people's stuff, it ranks just above trash in terms of its LACK of importance to her! Note to the wise, keep your stuff out of her purse!

The remainder of this chapter explores each of the top 30 product categories in detail from most common to least common.

Finance: 99%

Nearly every respondent in this study carries some items of a financial nature. Wallets, credit cards, debit cards and other bank information comprise the types of items frequently carried. Women who are married, college-educated and with higher incomes are more likely to carry credit cards and carry more types of cards. Those who frequently use coupons are more likely to carry store-brand credit cards, indicating a higher level of shopping involvement than the average respondent. Women who carry heavier bags with a higher number of items are more likely to carry credit cards and a checkbook.

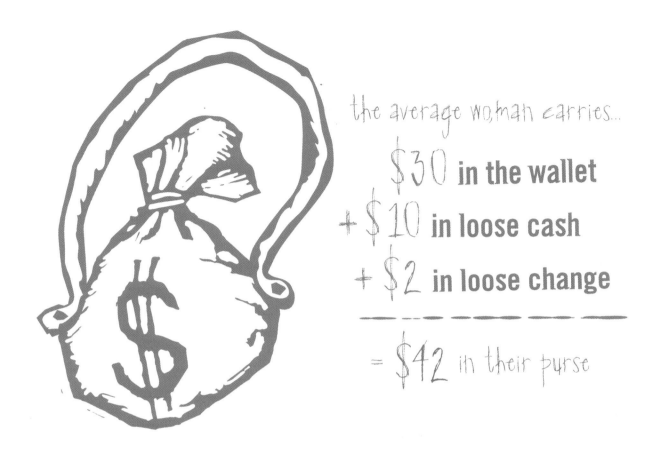

the average wo,man carries...

$30 **in the wallet**

+ $10 **in loose cash**

+ $2 **in loose change**

_____

= $42 in their purse

Conversely, smaller bags are less likely to carry a checkbook and more likely to carry loose cash in their purse, perhaps due to space constraints.

Women carry $42 on average in their purse: $30 in the wallet, if they have one, $10 in cash loose in the purse or in a pocket and about $2 in loose change. SIDE POCKETS 0 19 had $16.28 in change in her purse — one third the total weight of the bag. HIDDEN CHANGE 059 had a gob of loose change that had slipped between the purse and the lining inside. It was trapped and we couldn't find the hole, so we couldn't retrieve it to count it. Change is accumulated over time and rarely accessed at retail. It's typically spent in a lump sum or dumped into some type of container at home to be dealt with later. An enterprising retailer might develop a system that stores change under $1 on a reward card. Upon next purchase, the reward card would apply that change as a discount on a purchase, acting almost like a gift card. This rewards the customer and removes cost from the retail system in terms of coin management.

Reward Cards and Memberships: 98%

The Rewards and Memberships category is comprised of video/club cards, retail reward cards, punch cards for frequent buyers, library and gift cards. Nearly all respondents in this study carried some type of membership documentation in their purse. Retail reward cards are carried by nearly three out of every four respondents. This is followed closely by membership cards for video or club stores. Blockbuster Video tops the list of specific brands, but is overshadowed by the total collection of punch cards for frequent purchases, most often for local merchants. Keychain cards are prevalent.

Given the numbers of cards carried, they contribute significantly to complexity and clutter in the purse. Alternatives to cards would be appreciated by women to streamline transactions and improve findability in the purse.

"Why is it in a world where women claim to be so busy they can't breathe, that they carry so few planners and calendars? Only about one in six carry some type of time management tool, yet for those who carry them, it's a very important item. This seems like an area ripe with innovation opportunity."

Office Supplies: 93%

Almost every respondent had some type of office supply in her purse. Pens and other writing utensils are the most commonly carried items. Promotional pens from companies or various sources are the most common type of pen. Pencils, on the other hand, are rarely branded. Pens and Pencils are frequently "stolen" — lifted from merchants or even friends inadvertently. Women are frequently surprised by the number of writing tools in their purse.

Scraps of paper or notes and lists are the next most common office supply type item, typically carried to remind the respondent of important information. Unfortunately, these scraps are frequently discarded with the bag and forgotten. They become trash that clutters the bag. This suggests opportunity for information management that could be leveraged by personal technology devices.

Beauty/Hair Care: 91%

Beauty Care is one of the most extensive categories represented in the average purse. It consists of cosmetics, cosmetic accessories, fragrances, moisturizing lotions, and hair care items. Lip cosmetics lead the way in terms of beauty care items in the purse. This is followed closely by hair care items and accessories. One in five women carry fragrances in their purse, which is similar to the level that carry lotions and skin and eye cosmetics. Very few carry nail polish.

Though cosmetics overall were in the top five most important items less than ten percent of the time, there were very few bags without a lip product of some type (14% without). Even the smallest bag included at least one lip product.

Many of these products were purchased in attractive packages that over time were abraded and soiled,

with peeling labels, removing brand appeal and in some cases brand identification as well. This indicates an innovation opportunity for both packaging and printing technology.

One in five women carry a brush and/or comb for grooming. Importantly, there were no styling products in any of the purses researched. This likely represents opportunity for innovation.

For almost half of those carrying a cosmetic accessory, that accessory was a makeup bag. This bag within a bag is symptomatic of organizational issues and compensatory behavior to collect loose items into "findable" units in the purse.

One in three purses contain a moisturizing lotion – principally for hand and body use. Very few facial moisturizing products were observed. While some lotions may have contained sunscreen, this is clearly not a prevalent behavior or recognized benefit yet. This is an area for innovation opportunity.

One in five women carries a fragrance in her purse. Most impressive was the fact that many of the fragrances observed were in full-size containers – not smaller travel sizes. Fragrances tended to be light in potency, like body mist or spray. Very few high-end, designer fragrances were observed in purses.

Nearly a third of all purses contain some type of skin cosmetics. Powder/compacts top the list with nearly one out of every four women carrying it in her purse. Foundation, concealer and blush round out the other top skin cosmetics in the bag. These items are considered "touchups" for use throughout the day.

One in four purses contains at least one eye-specific cosmetic product. Eye liner/pencil and Mascara are common to one in five bags with eye shadow slightly less prevalent.

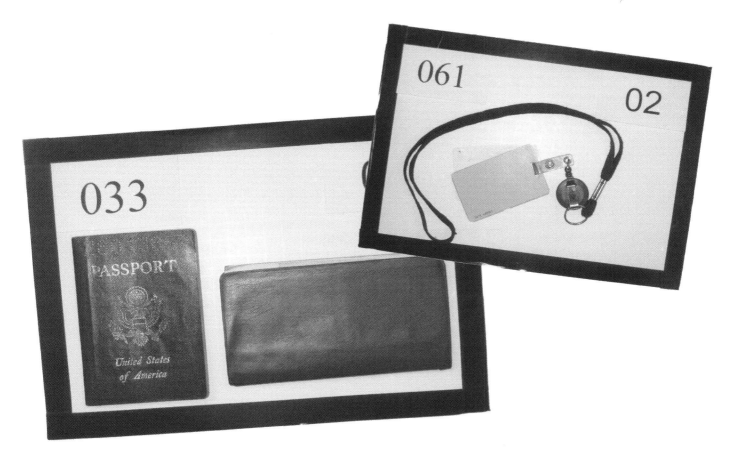

Identification: 91%

Most women in this study carried some type of personal identification. Surprisingly, nearly ten percent did not carry personally identifying documentation in their purse or on their person while out in public. This indicates a certain confidence on the part of the consumer and a potential lack of security regarding the use of credit cards if retailers cannot verify identification for all card users.

Most identification is in the form of a Driver's License. About half carry other identifying documents, most frequently a social security card. ID badges for employment, school or other purposes are carried about as often. We found a few women carrying original Birth Certificates around, but this was pretty rare.

Very few respondents used a specialized ID holder. This may be an opportunity for innovation to help respondents quickly and easily retrieve identification when needed.

"Interestingly, women carry keys and key chains in great big gobs. One had so many keys I wondered if she was running a jail."

Security and Access: 86% (Car Lock/Remote: 19%)

More than four out of five respondents carried keys — makes you wonder how the other 18% get into their homes, cars and offices! Car lock fobs (electronic openers) are carried by nearly one in five women in this study. Garage-door openers were carried in purses by 2% of women in this study. ID badges are included in this section because they give access to the workplace via bar codes or electronic swipe readers. They are carried by one in five women in their purses.

Interestingly, women carry keys and key chains in great big gobs. MORE IS MORE 043 had so many keys I wondered if she was running a jail. Women frequently use the sound of the keychain, while shaking their purse, to locate their keys. Key Chains are often adorned with sentimental items, souvenirs and gift keepsakes that remind them of happy times or important people. Innovation in this area would focus on what could help women streamline their keychain, yet find keys quickly, or eliminate the need for keys altogether.

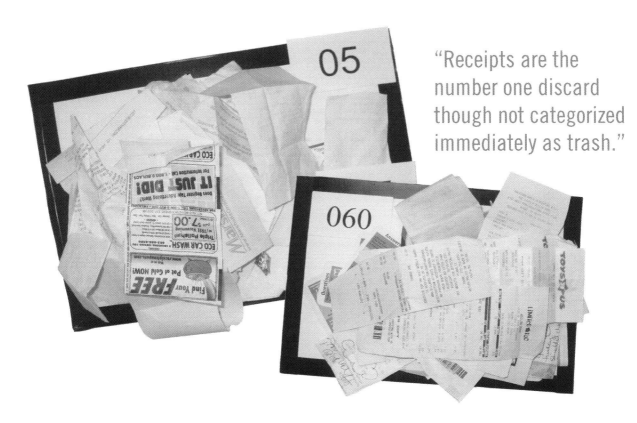

"Receipts are the number one discard though not categorized immediately as trash."

Receipts: 85%

Women carry receipts in their purses and hold onto them somewhat compulsively. In fact, I found one dated 2001 in this study! Most often these are stuffed into a wallet or pocket, or even floating loose in the bag. Over time, these receipts become outdated, damaged and degrade into trash. When they are disposed of, it is en masse, as the bag is cleaned and restored to greater utility. Receipts are the number-one discard though not categorized immediately as trash. It's only after she examines it closely for the date, transaction type, and likelihood to need it in the future. Then, it becomes trash, with nearly one third of all purses containing a receipt that became trash during the interview.

Most receipts carried in the purse are miscellaneous in nature, deriving from a wide variety of sources. Those that are identifiable as a groups include Club Stores, Grocery Stores, and Department Stores.

Cell Phones/Accessories: 74%

Nearly three quarters of all purses contained cell phones and many also held sometype of phone accessory such as a charger, ear pieces, etc. The most common brands of cell phone included Motorola, Samsung and Nokia.

Some women carried their cell phones in an external pocket of the bag for easy, fast access. Others used very loud ring tones as a way to locate the phone if it was floating loose in the bag. Yet others had purchased a pouch for the phone that clipped or connected to the bag. All of these behaviors suggest both the importance of the cell phone, the premium placed on quick access when needed, and how women compensate for its shortcomings in terms of findability.

Insurance: 71%

Nearly three quarters of all respondents in this study carried insurance documentation in their purses. Medical/Dental topped the list of types of items carried for insurance purposes. This is probably due to the more frequent access required than for auto insurance, which is often carried in the automobile itself.

Many respondents also carried insurance paperwork in their purses either as proof of insurance (medical) or to follow up on issues noted in the paperwork. In many cases, these important items are damaged and difficult to read. This suggests innovation opportunity.

Food, Gum, Candy: 63%

More than half of all women with purses carry some type of food item. This is most often a mint, candy or gum item — though more than 5% carry some type of bar product, like a granola bar.

The purse is almost like a mobile pantry, yet doesn't contain much actual, nutritious food, or meaningful amounts of beverages. And woman cannot live on gum alone! Innovation is as much about what's not in the purse as it is about what's in it. This suggests innovation opportunity for highly efficient foods/beverages or nutritive gums/mints that offer filling, nutritious, on-the-go benefits with little weight/bulk in the bag.

Candy and Gum wrappers are the most common trash items carried in purses. Packaging innovation for these categories should address the elimination of wrappers that become trash. They poorly represent the brand long term and cause an annoyance for the user base of these products.

Healthcare: 61%

Many women who carry a purse carry at least one Healthcare item. The vast majority of these items are medications, either prescription or over-the-counter. Pain medications top the list of remedies carried in the purse.

"Many prescription bottles were unmarked and unlabeled and contain unidentifiable medications..."

Many prescription bottles were unmarked and unlabeled and contain unidentifiable medications, perhaps even illegal drugs. It was not possible to make that determination in the interviews. One out of every ten respondents had at least one loose pill in the purse, which was typically discarded at the end of the interview along with other trash.

Birth control pills were carried by 6% of respondents, but only 2% carried condoms — suggesting perhaps that pregnancy may be a greater concern than sexually transmitted disease.

Packaging and organization of medical items could solve important problems for women including safety, hygiene, identification of medications and the ability to find these critical products when they're needed.

Coupons: 61%

One in three respondents used coupons for more than half of their grocery trips. Yet, coupons are carried by nearly two thirds of respondents. This suggests opportunity for innovative approaches to "couponing" and coupon-carrying mechanisms.

Brand coupons are underrepresented in purses suggesting that they are not as appealing as store coupons or those for other outlets such as restaurants (coded as various).

Coupons were a frequent "discard" during the course of these interviews. Almost one in ten women threw a coupon in the trash when their interview was complete. Most often this was due to expiration, but it was sometimes due to the interest waning between the clipping of the coupon and the opportunity to redeem it.

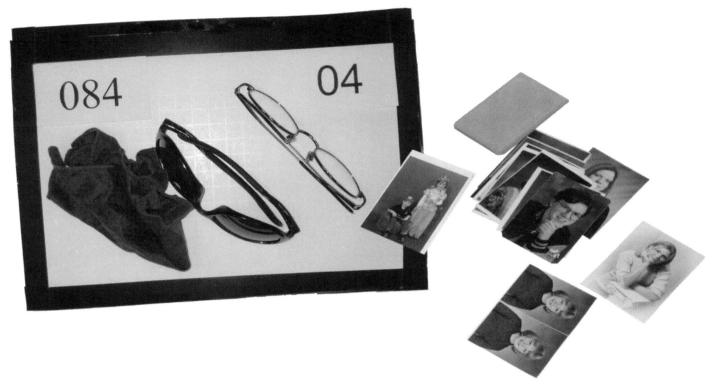

Eye Care: 61%

More than half of respondents carried items for vision care in their purse. Sunglasses were by far the most common vision-care item, carried by a full 40% of women in this study. Eye glasses were carried by about a third and nearly one is six carried eye drops. Eye-care items require special care in the harsh and unsanitary environment of the purse and so are generally in some type of case/holder. Sunglasses are not always stored in this way and so are subject to damage and wear, both aesthetically as well as lens damage that can affect product performance.

Photographs: 59%

A full 60% of total respondents carried photographs in their purses. Generally, these are photographs of loved ones, often children, either their own or the children of other family members. Photographs are keepsakes that capture memories and are carried for many years. Unfortunately, most of them are not enjoyed often because they are stuffed in wallets behind credit cards and other items. In fact, very few are kept in any type of photo holder or case. Many women rediscovered photographs (they'd forgotten

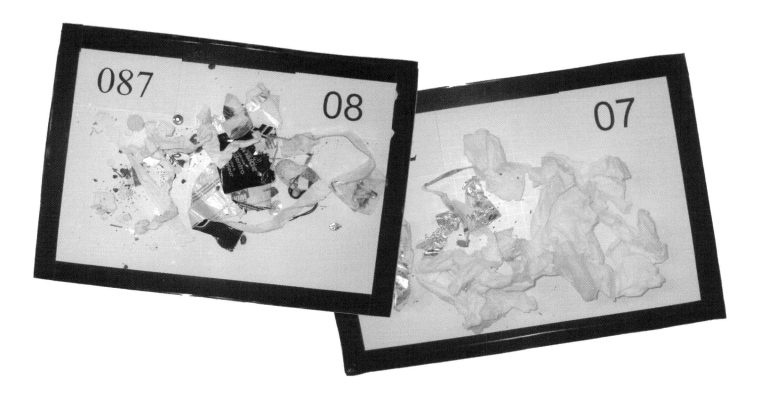

about) during their interviews and this was emotional for them. Wouldn't it be great if there were ways to hold, store and show photographs within the context of the purse? In fact, what if the wallet had transparent pockets on the outside for photographs? That way, women could enjoy these precious mementos more often.

Trash & Scrap Paper: 51%

Trash was accounted for in two ways in this study. First, we asked women to designate a pile for trash. This tended to include obvious things like gum and candy wrappers, loose tobacco, straw wrappers and other debris, typically made of paper. About half of all women in this study could create such a pile.

Then, as the interview progressed, the respondents would add discards — what they wanted to throw away at the end of the interview — to the trash pile. Total discards weighed two ounces on average because again, they were principally made of paper. The key difference was that while wrappers are trash automatically after the item is unwrapped, other things become trash over time. Specifically, coupons

"purse trash

tended to include obvious things like gum and candy wrappers...and other debris, typically made of paper. While wrappers are trash automatically after the item is unwrapped, other things become trash over time."

expire, receipts become irrelevant as time passes, and other items just don't survive the wear & tear of the purse environment and become trash as a result. Cough drops, pens & pencils, and even tampons that accidentally come unwrapped, all begin their journey in the purse as useful and end up as trash because they can't withstand the harsh treatment. What can innovators learn from trash? Packages that dispense product without leaving wrappers behind and products that are packaged in such a way that they protect the product until the moment of use are two of many potential avenues to pursue.

Jewelry: 40%

A full 40% of women carried jewelry in their handbags. Most often, however, it is not carried for some sort of emergency accessorizing! Rather, it is forgotten and often broken. The purse is a place to store the jewelry until it can be fixed or stored at home in a more appropriate place. Even though we found single earrings and clearly damaged/destroyed items, no respondent discarded any jewelry items as trash during the interview.

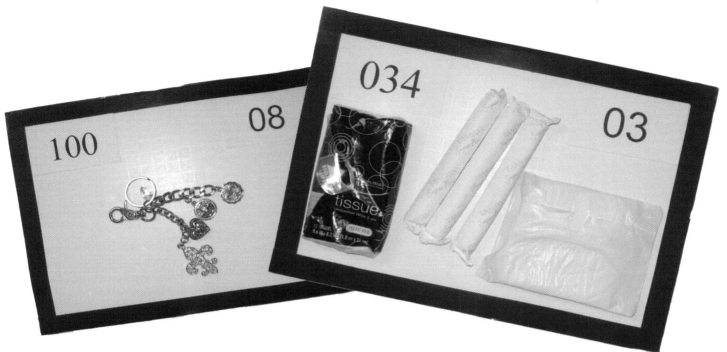

Nail Care: 31%

Nail files and clippers were carried by close to one third of all women in their purses. Nail polish was carried by only 4% of all respondents. This suggests that the occasions for nail care are quick touch-up or damage repair and not beautifying moments. How could nail polish or even nail decorating be made more portable and appropriate on-the-go? This could open doors for innovative new products.

Feminine Care: 28%

One in four women carried tampons or pads in their purses. This number is surprisingly low given the numbers of women who claim that the need for feminine protection is why they first started carrying a purse. It may be that women don't carry them all the time, but only in anticipation of need during certain weeks/days a month. But, equally likely is the fact that keeping these products in the purse long-term leads to damage and lack of usefulness in the "moment of truth." The wrappers used to enclose tampons and pads are thin and flimsy. This is probably because they're sold in boxes that protect them well enough for in-home use. This same packaging provides insufficient protection long-term in the purse.

Tissues: 27%

One in four women carried facial tissues, sometimes in packages, but more often loose or in sandwich bags from home. There are many, many dirty, torn, unsanitary and useless tissues in purses. A full 6% of women discarded tissues at the end of our interview, but most stuffed them right back in the bag. This suggests that the tissue is considered important by those who carry them, but insufficiently protected so women compensate by bringing their own bags, or just tossing them out when they become too grimy to use. This situation offers many avenues for package innovation in this category.

Smoking Items: 24%

Cigarettes and/or accessories were carried by nearly one out of every four respondents in this study. Matches and lighters outpaced cigarettes, however, which is a paradox of sorts. Many women admitted that they replaced a lighter they thought was lost, then found both during our interview.

Two of our 100 respondents carried rolling papers in their purses, so it's possible that lighters are used to light things other than tobacco!

Loose tobacco debris was observed in 3% of all purses, or 13% of those who carry smoking items. The women who observed their own loose tobacco tumbling onto the table were embarrassed by the lack of cleanliness this created.

"How many unclean things in the purse do you touch while rummaging for your hand sanitizer?"

Hand Sanitizers/Moist Wipes/Skin Cleaners: 23%

About one in four carried a cleansing product for personal use. Hand sanitizer outpaced moist wipes by about 50%. This suggests a strong need to clean hands without water. But, how easy is it to find these products when they're needed? How many unclean things in the purse do you touch while rummaging for your hand sanitizer?

Food/Drink Supplies: 23%

Almost one in four respondents carried an eating or drinking implement of some type. Most of these were napkins or toothpicks, but a few were carrying utensils, straws and even bottle openers in their purses. All of these items are susceptible to the unclean environment of the purse. Some of them were wrapped, like disposable utensils and straws, but they were not wrapped well and most were unwrapped.

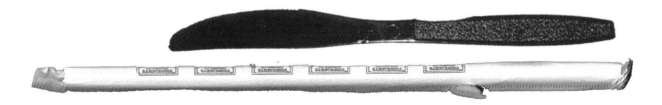

Oral Care: 22%

Oral-care items were carried by one in five respondents in their purses. Dental floss was the most common item, but toothbrushes, breath strips and even tooth wipes were found. Almost none were in any type of protected, closed package. This exposes things you commonly put in your mouth to the many germs that are carried on your hands as you access items in the purse and bacteria in the purse itself. Eeewww. Toothbrushes were the item most likely to be carried in a plastic sandwich bag.

Religious Items: 15%

Items of religious significance were carried in a modest number of purses. These take the form of Rosaries, Funeral Cards, Medals, Crosses and even notes from Bible-Study classes. Most of these items were carried as reminders or tokens, but not necessarily for ready access or daily use.

Weapons: 14%

A full 14% of women in this study carried items that could be considered weapons and the knife was the weapon of choice. Several of these knives were more of the utility variety (Swiss Army), but more often

than not, these knives were carried for protection. Other items carried for protection included flashlights and pepper spray, but at much lower levels.

This is interesting because a knife is such an intimate way to defend yourself. You have to be very close to someone to use a knife for protection. Are there better ways to protect yourself? Yes. Are they designed for a woman's needs and more importantly, are they designed for ready access in her purse? Probably not -- yet.

Personal Technology: 13%

More than one in ten women carried some form of personal technology in their purses. These items typically took two forms: electronic storage media and MP3 Players, categorized here as electronic accessories. Innovation opportunities could include dust/dirt protection and crush-proof storage. Functionality of these products could be further leveraged to replace scrap paper and other information-collection methods. These devices could also help keep track of a woman's schedule since very few are carrying planners or calendars. These devices, as they exist today, were not designed specifically to meet the needs of women who carry purses. This is fertile ground for innovation.

Keepsakes: 10%

Many women carried irreplaceable keepsakes and mementos in their purses. They perceive this as a safe place, and yet purses are lost and stolen every day. When a purse is stolen, it is the personal keepsakes that are missed as other things can be replaced.

Keepsakes are frequently damaged or destroyed and not accessed often for enjoyment. That's because they're stuffed in a wallet or pocket for safekeeping. Could there be innovation opportunity to help women showcase and enjoy their keepsakes while keeping them in their purse? Could there be security systems to alert women when their purse was moving away from them via theft of just left behind accidentally?

Cameras & Accessories: 8%

Cameras and camera accessories were carried by only a handful of respondents. Disposable cameras were outpaced by digital options by more than 2 to 1. Given the numbers of photographs in the purse, does this suggest opportunity for digital-photo capture and display in a single device? Could this device be integrated with others? Certainly cell phones have begun to deliver on this, but picture quality is poor and displays are too small to enjoy readily. There are many innovation avenues to explore for this category.

10.

Same Difference

While people are, in their essence, infinitely complex and limitless in their individualism, we tend to have more things in common than we have differences. That's why a study like this can delve deeply to understand a few people, 100 in this case, and draw fairly accurate conclusions about society at large. Then again, there are some sub-groups who think, feel and behave very differently from the general population. If we only look at the total group, we can miss some of these differences because they're diluted in the "melting pot" so to speak. By examining differences between these groups and the total sample, we can pick up on overlooked cues and gain a unique understanding that can inspire innovative thinking.

For this study – ten sub-groups are examined in detail, including:

1) **Age Groups** (18–34, 35–44, 45–64)
2) **Income Levels** (<$50k, $50 – 99k, $100k+)
3) **Households with Kids** (moms)
4) **Race/Ethnicity** (caucasian vs non-caucasian)
5) **Coupon Users** (frequent vs infrequent users)
6) **Type of Purse** (segments previously defined)
7) **Size of Purse** (small, medium, large)
8) **Weight of Purse** (<2lbs, 3–4 lbs, 4+lbs)
9) **Frequency of Changing Purse** (weekly, monthly/quarterly, <quarterly)
10) **Number of Items in Purse** (1–29, 30–59, 60+)

Five comparisons were considered:

1) Reasons women like this particular purse carried on the day of the interview.
2) Bag Statistics (weight, measurements, number of items, bag type)
3) Five most important items in the purse.
4) Percent of grocery trips responsible for making.
5) Weekly grocery spending.

For each group, only key differences and highlights are presented.

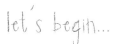

Age Group Summary

While all age groups value the color or design of their purses, older age groups tend to skew toward more practicality than younger age groups. There is a resurgence toward trendy, smaller bags in later age groups, once the responsibility for children and other family members eases. Bags also become small again at this stage in life.

Middle age groups carry the greatest number of items and have heavier bags. They skew toward "tote" designs. They also consider a broader range of items to be 'important' perhaps indicating the responsibility that extends beyond themselves to children and family and the higher need for preparedness at this life stage.

Income Summary:

While lower-income groups express strong preferences for color and design in their purses, they steer clear of Bling designs, skewing toward more practical purses. Higher income groups tend to have heavier bags with more items in them. They also spend more on groceries per week and tend to use coupons less frequently than other income groups.

Mom Summary:

Women with children in the household (moms) have larger purses that are heavier and have more items in them. However, when asked what they liked about their purses, this group tended to skew toward color and design, perhaps delighting in the simple joy of this personal item in their lives. Women without children in the household list many practical reasons for liking their purse including: ergonomics, pockets, durability, etc.

Ethnic Group Summary:

The sample in this study is balanced to represent non-Caucasian groups as a whole (African American, Hispanic, and Asian) at census levels. However, this provides too few interviews to look at each race and ethnic group separately. Therefore, the three race and ethnic groups are combined as non-Caucasian and compared to the Caucasian sample for general learning purposes.

Non-Caucasian groups are much more likely than Caucasians to cite design and color as a reason to like a purse — yet they are much LESS likely to be carrying a Bling style purse. Carrying identification is much more important to non-Caucasian groups than Caucasians. Perhaps this suggests more scrutiny of their identity in society (my hypothesis).

"Three quarters of frequent coupon users are over the age of 35, suggesting that coupon use is aging. This raises important questions for marketers and retailers regarding how to reach younger age groups with effective transactional discount tools."

Coupon User Summary:

Coupon Users were divided into *frequent*, those who used coupons for more than half of their grocery trips, and *infrequent*, those who rarely/never used coupons when they shop. This simple, two-tier division of the sample yielded enough interviews for analdysis.

Frequent coupon users tend to prefer more durable purses with more pockets. They also tend to carry bigger purses with more items in them. Three quarters of frequent coupon users are over the age of 35, suggesting that coupon use is aging. This raises important questions for marketers and retailers regarding how to reach younger age groups with effective transactional discount tools. Frequent coupon users spend less per week on groceries than Infrequent coupon users. This probably does not suggest that coupons lower their overall grocery bill, but probably indicates that heavy coupon users are looking for and employing a variety of methods to keep their grocery spending low – or they really need the savings to help make ends meet in the household.

Purse Type Summary:

This section is presented on the basis of qualitative analysis and should be used with caution as base sizes were very small for some types of purses. The eight types of purses examined included: Sausage, Micro Bag, External Pocket, Slouch, Tote, Bling, Upscale Print and Mini Backpack.

Upscale Print and External Pocket purses tend to be larger than others, yet neither style holds the greatest number of items. This honor belongs to the Sausage bag, holding 89 items on average. Micro Bags place more importance on cash than others, probably because they're too small to hold a wallet in most cases. Upscale Print owners claim to that brand is not important, yet it's featured prominently all over the bag. This suggests that brand is important, but not something they really want to admit. Backpack owners tend to think every item is equally important. Maybe that's why they need a backpack?

Purse Size Summary:

Who says size doesn't matter? Only someone who carries a small purse! Like a self-fulfilling prophecy, a bag's size determines how much it is liked for its size. For example, larger purses are liked as much for the size as for the color or design. This isn't the case with smaller purses, where size is often a dislike (too small).

Duh. Larger purses weight more and contain more items. Women who carry larger purses claim to do more of the grocery shopping. And, they tend to be Sausage shaped (the purse, that is), or have external pockets attached.

Small purses place a stronger emphasis on cash and credit cards, where larger bags contain wallets that hold these things.

Purse Weight Summary:

Women who carry heavier purses tend to have more responsibility for grocery shopping and spend more per week on groceries. That may explain why their bags have more emphasis on compartments and pockets to keep things organized. Not surprisingly, their purses also contain more items, so not all of the additional weight is the bag itself.

Women who carry lighter purses tend to value ergonomics more than those who carry heavier purses.

Frequency of Changing Purses Summary:

Women who change the purse they're carrying frequently, do so based on the color or design of the purse. Women who rarely change their purses, like the size of the purse equally as much as its appearance. They also value ergonomics. This suggests that the appeal of color and design is more fleeting and that loyalty is driven by satisfying practical concerns. Or, it could indicate that there are some women for whom matching their outfit with the right purse is of the utmost importance. Ideally, a purse that balanced the color and design with practical features would inspire loyal usage.

Number of Items in the Purse Summary:

Women who carry large numbers of items in their purses claim to like the color and design more than anything else about the bag. Yet, they also strongly value extra compartments and large-size bags. Let's face it, they just want it all!

Sausage-style bags are carried by this group more frequently than other types of purses, perhaps due to the visibility of items inside offered by the wide mouth and the shallow depth that allows light to penetrate.

Those with large numbers of items are more likely to carry a wallet and/or checkbook, contributing additional nooks and crannies for stuffing things. And, those carrying more items tend toward more responsibility for grocery shopping and spend more on groceries per week than others in this study.

color & design

practical features

Ideally, a purse that balanced the color and design with practical features would inspire loyal usage.

contradiction
is where the genius
of innovation lies.

11.

The Purse as a Catalyst for Innovation

I always get really hungry when I swim. I think this probably happens to a lot of people, but I'm acutely aware of it myself because I'm rarely hungry. Most Americans eat because they're in the habit of it or because they enjoy eating. We rarely allow ourselves to become hungry.

Have you ever noticed how much more appealing even the simplest food is when you're really hungry? I once spent five hours on the tarmac on an airplane at LaGuardia. By hour three, I was as hungry as I'd ever been, even after swimming. I fished things out of the bottom of my purse and briefcase to eat, including gum that was so old and fragile it broke into dust and pieces when unwrapped, cough drops with the label so firmly affixed I ate the label, and graham cracker dust in a cellophane bag that was formerly graham crackers a year or so before. When you are really hungry, you can see the value in food that you may not have seen before.

Contradiction is where the genius of innovation lies. This chapter reveals contradictions that inspire and offers product ideas as a springboard for your own thinking. The innovator can identify unmet and unarticulated needs by paying homage to the contradictions observed and build products to satisfy these needs. The first company to do that will win a spot in the purse and in the woman's heart as a consumer. Let's explore some contradictions observed and identify some innovation opportunities in the process.

contradiction #1: indispensable organizational tool that is a mobile junk drawer

The purse is considered a vital and indispensable tool that keeps a woman organized throughout her day. Yet, it's a disorganized mess. Things are jumbled and piled, rummaged through and rifled several

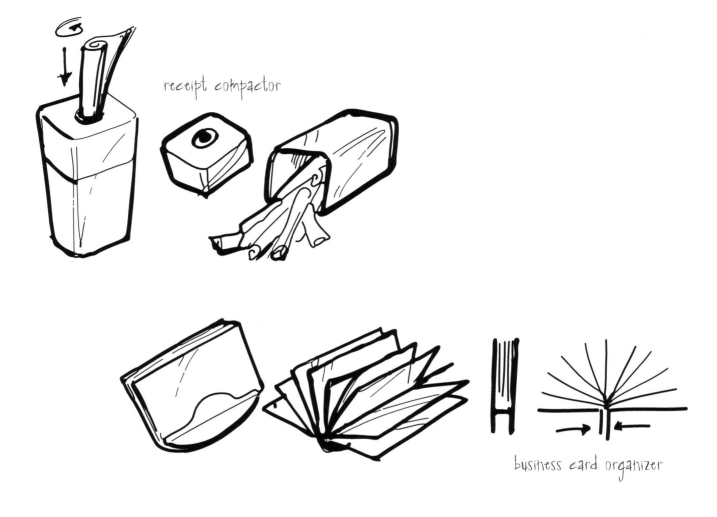

receipt compactor

business card organizer

minutes at a time to find or not find that one thing she was sure was in there. It is the very essence of disorganization. Imagine that you use a file drawer to keep all of your important papers and that these papers keep you organized throughout your day. Yet, nothing is actually filed. It's just thrown in the drawers at random and the entire contents rifled each time you needed a specific piece of paper. There are unmet needs here! We know this from the extraordinary lengths women go to in trying to make a few key items readily "findable" like huge key chains and wallets attached with a string. Innovation opportunity spans the range from the purse itself to container companies and categories that want to make themselves more findable via specialized packaging.

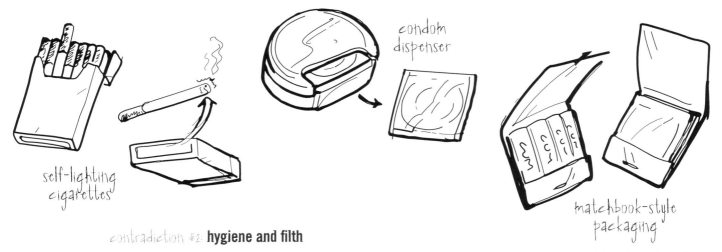

self-lighting cigarettes

condom dispenser

matchbook-style packaging

contradiction #2: **hygiene and filth**

A woman's bag contains an almost limitless array of things you put in your mouth: toothbrushes, dental floss, cigarettes, toothpicks, lipsticks – and yet it is an environment that is never actually cleaned. It's assumed to be relatively clean when purchased and occasionally emptied of extraneous items and trash, but it's never really disinfected or scrubbed free of the dirt and grime of daily living. This was not consciously recognized by the respondents in this research. Innovation opportunity spans the gamut from products that clean the purse to purses that don't get dirty to sub-containers for things that go in your mouth that you want to keep clean.

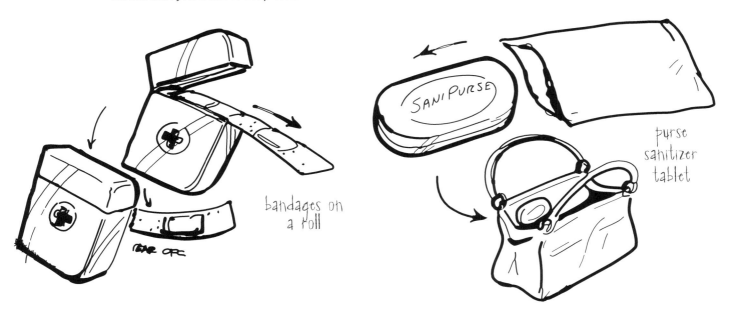

bandages on a roll

SANIPURSE

purse sanitizer tablet

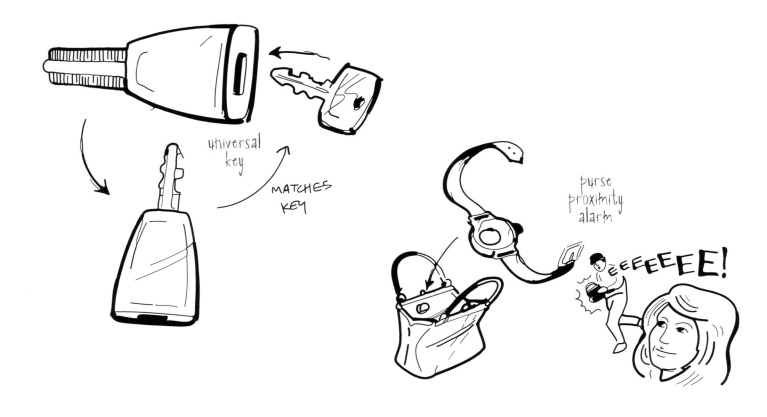

universal key

MATCHES KEY

purse proximity alarm

EEEEEEEE!

contradiction #3: **safety deposit box that's easily left behind or stolen**

Women perceive their purse as a sanctuary for precious things, both rational as in the financial instruments of daily life, and emotional, as in the keepsakes from their son's wedding ten years ago. Given the sanctity of the item in terms of its privacy rules and general proximity to a woman's body, the purse is considered the appropriate place to store things of importance. Yet, it is a poor object for this purpose given its lack of locking mechanisms and opportunity to become lost, separated, or stolen from its owner. Innovation opportunity could include things that secure the bag and things that secure its proximity to the owner. Locator devices could also prove useful on a daily basis as many women do not have a specific place where the purse is stored in the home between uses. Simple daily locating is a huge unmet need.

contradiction #4: **the most vital things in life and trash, trash, trash**

A woman's purse is the bank where she deposits the most important things in life. Yet it is also a wasteland of trash and debris. Generally paper and broken things, the trash contents do not weigh very much, perhaps one to two ounces per bag, but the volume is staggering. Sometimes, when pulled out and piled up, the trash is actually larger than the purse, suggesting magnificent compaction on the part of the owner. Old receipts, expired coupons and candy/gum wrappers are the most common trash items. At a minimum, innovators in the trash-management industries could develop specialized containers and bags for this. Moreover, companies that make trash-producing items (candy, gum, tampons, etc.) could invent specific purse packs for their products that self-manage trash, thus keeping trash from entering the purse entirely.

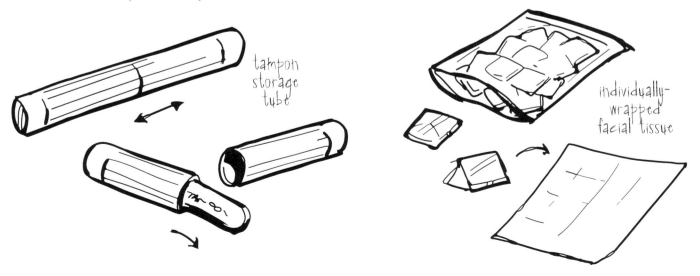

tampon storage tube

individually-wrapped facial tissue

beverage holster

voice-activated
list maker

contradiction #5: **frequently used essentials and forgotten, broken things**

"Oh my gosh, I wondered where that was!"—was a very common expression during these interviews. While women readily profess that this bag is an indispensable vessel holding frequently used essential items, they almost always stumble across a piece of broken jewelry that needed to go to the shop ages ago. Also, because the environment in the bag is unstable—things are piled in randomly and the bag itself is tossed from car seat to shoulder to retail counter to car seat again. Things are often broken and disheveled, sometimes becoming inadvertent trash in the process. Innovation opportunity could range from making the items themselves more durable or designing a more rational environment.

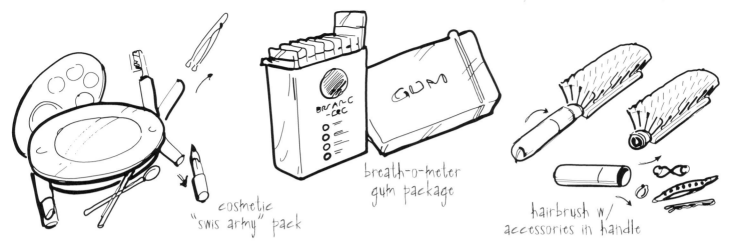

cosmetic
"swis army" pack

breath-o-meter
gum package

hairbrush w/
accessories in handle

contradiction #: **cosmetics that beautify yet do not maintain their own beauty**

The purse is a mobile makeup counter, used for touchups or complete application when necessary to do so. Yet, the makeup itself is stored in such a harsh environment that it becomes very unattractive as a set of tools to beautify. Labels are dirty and scratched off. Product is leaking around the seals, damaging not only the product itself, but other bag contents as well. Brushes are filled with debris you probably wouldn't want in your hair or eyelashes or brushed across your skin. Some women use a separate makeup bag, but this just concentrates the problem in an isolated environment. While an improvement, since your mascara isn't brushing up against loose changes and gum wrappers, it's still not displaying the products and maintaining the packages in a way conducive to the brand essence of elegance and beauty.

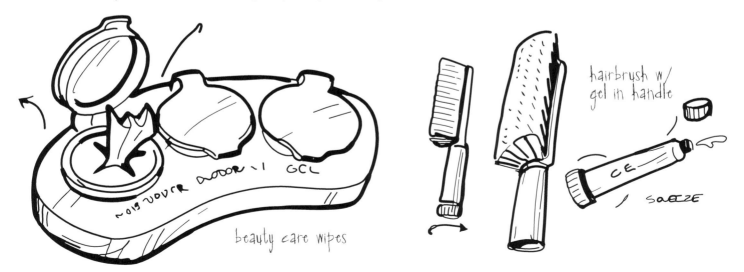

beauty care wipes

hairbrush w/
gel in handle

squeeze

contradiction #7: **irreplaceable things stored in a damaging, unsafe environment**

Beneath the wallet, in the bowels of the last pocket on the right, is a secret treasure trove. It's been there for many years and traveled the space from purse to purse. It holds a woman's heart through her history. Keepsakes and treasures are stored in the purse for two reasons:

1) to keep them safe and close by, and
2) so that she can randomly visit them and rekindle a happy moment in her memory.

Fortunes from fortune cookies, wedding mementos, photographs, prayer cards, old jewelry and countless other artifacts make up this group of irreplaceable items. Yet, they're often sandwiched between credit cards and lists of errands to run, or stuffed in a forgotten pocket that's difficult to actually visit with any frequency to meet emotional needs. Innovators in the keepsake industries should be encouraged that this phenomenon occurs outside the home and yet opportunities lie in the lack of security, organization, display and access these items have in the environment of the purse.

keepsake wallet

"THESE ARE THE PRIMARY CONTRADICTIONS, but there are many, many more. For every category of items in the purse there is a host of contradictions to explore — and with this a wealth of innovation opportunity to make the lives of women more conducive to actual living and the innovator's achievement, bringing new and different products to the market that delight consumers into buying them. Ah, it's a perfect match."

how how did that get in here?

you know, it's a funny story. i have this friend...

12.

I Can't Believe That's in my Purse

She tried to pass it off as a parking ticket, but the word "solicitation" was clearly emblazoned on the top of the summons. While we didn't see any other evidence of illegal activity, there were plenty of surprises in store and the most common reaction from the respondent was "I can't believe that's in my purse."

Among the unexpected things we found were an entire class of items I call "other people's stuff." This included a friend's wallet, stuffed animals, a T-shirt, a plastic cowboy, and even the empty package from a male enhancement herb. At the end of the interview, I asked COCK STAR 94, "Well, uhn, how did things work out with that enhancement product? Did it work?" Her entire body slumped in the chair and she uttered a disappointed "no." When respondents were asked to rank items by importance, "other people's stuff" ranked second only to trash in its LACK of importance to them.

OLIVE OIL 100 mentioned that she was feeling a little down on her luck. So, her mother suggested that she carry olive oil to "bless" the things around her. She took what looked like a child's bubble-blowing toy, complete with bubble wand, and filled it with oil for this purpose. She seemed very happy with the results, having blessed her home, her car and many other things around her. She may be on to something.

We found letters from loved ones, near and far, and even one letter from the local penitentiary. The return address: "Big Pussy Mama." And, we found an assortment of items purportedly from a bachelorette party, including a penis-shaped pencil topper (try that around the office) and a portable sachet of personal lubricant (you never know).

There were no identifiable illegal drugs, but there were rolling papers and lighters in purses without cigarettes, so that math's pretty simple. And, about a third of all purses contained prescription bottles, or other unidentifiable medication containers, that could be used to hide drugs. About 10% of all purses had loose pills rambling around in the bottom and they could have been anything, frankly. Given the fact that most of them were disposed of after the interview, they probably weren't illegal.

The filth in some of these purses was indescribable — as was the odor. I went through two entire containers of antibacterial wipes cleaning my hands and the work surface between every interview. There were gobs of hair, mixed with open, gooey cough drops, loose tobacco and unidentifiable clumps of yuck. One woman carried crystals wrapped in a scarf. When she removed them and shook the scarf, she created a cloud of dust we can only hope was from the crystals and not some type of contagion.

On the other hand, some women were clearly emotional when they found keepsakes, such as souvenirs from long-forgotten weddings or funerals, or photos of long-lost loved ones or babies fully grown now. It was touching to watch them look at the photos and flash through the memories, then tenderly place them back in their wallet, waiting for another future moment to remember.

13.

Mythology and the Man Bag

Let me start by saying that I haven't researched men and their relationships, passive or active, with purses, living, dead, or otherwise. So, from this point forward, you should assume that I'm making this up – as opposed to the rest of this book which is painstakingly researched and reliably compiled. But still, when it comes to the "Man Bag" these aren't thin-air conclusions I'm drawing. Rather, they're hypotheses drawn from available information, observation and experience living with men for more than 45 years. That said, I think I'm on pretty firm ground.

Men, in general, do not carry purses – at least not in a traditional sense. A purse is defined as an object used to carry a variety of items in order to be prepared for any given situation a person might encounter on a typical day. Instead, men carry objects used to carry a single, specific type of thing like business papers, tools, gym clothes, or lunch.

Perhaps key to this is that some categories of importance to women (cosmetics and feminine hygiene) are irrelevant to men. Perhaps men also have a lesser need to be the solution to other people's problems or choose only to solve those that can be solved with the contents of their pockets (wallet, pocket knife, handkerchief, or fist). If they need an adhesive bandage, they'll find a way to get one or buy one or just wait until they get home. They will not, in general, be appalled with themselves for not having an adhesive bandage at the moment the need arises.

i may be guessing here, but i think you're nodding your head "yes."

I think this phenomenon may go all the way back to hunters and gatherers. If modern man "hunts" through his day, he carries only the tool he needs at that particular moment. He has his wallet and can hunt down an adhesive bandage if he needs one. On the other hand, if modern woman "gathers" her way through the day, or through her life, that would account for the accumulation effect of the purse. Contents aren't so much designed as they are accumulated over time, as various needs occur, and the result is vast numbers of items from a variety of categories that, in turn, prepare her for any needs that may arise in a lifetime of gathering people, projects, responsibilities, and opportunities to further gather. So, whether it's a purse for stuff or a big heart for kisses, she needs something to carry all the things gathered in a gathering life.

Two recent innovations offer intriguing new avenues for the development of men's bags:

1) the iPack Messenger Bag with built-in MP3 player, and
2) the IBM Trader Bag, a handheld device with holster.

Perhaps this idea of integrating technology is a way to make the bag itself more relevant overall for men. Technology may make the purse more permissible for men.

epilogue.

What's Next?

The first question people ask about this study is "How did you come up with this idea?"
The last question people ask about this study is "What's Next?"

Well, that's a tough one. I'd like to say that after doing this study, I want to study the surf from a far away beach, by blanket, preferably with a tall, frosty drink in hand. But, in reality, I'm infinitely curious and love the work I do.

So, there are three directions to go from here:

1) Make the data report "In Your Purse: Archaeology of the American Handbag" broadly available to help companies better understand women as a target group and their needs and motivations, not just specific to this study, but more broadly through other research.
2) Help companies better understand their product categories through custom analysis of this data set.
3) Help Innovators make the most of this study by facilitating Innovation Workshops, which are an important part of InsightFarm's Consumer Strategy Practice.
4) Create "In Your Car," "In Your Pantry," "In Your Garbage," or any number of limitless extensions of the study.

As a good friend once told me "When given a choice, take both!"

So, I've decided to pursue all of these avenues of discovery. If you'd like to learn more, please contact me. It's been a wild ride and it's been my pleasure to share it with you!

insightfarm

Consumer Knowledge
to Get you Growing

Insightfarm is a Market Research and Consumer
Strategy Consulting firm Dedicated to Driving
Business Growth through Consumer Insight.

Kelley Styring
Consumer Strategist

Helping formulate growth strategies and innovation
programs based on consumer insight for Fortune
100 companies for more than 10 years.

Kelley.styring@insightfarm.com
www.insightfarm.com
503-554-5567
19960 Ribbon Ridge Road,
Newberg, OR 97132

Printed in the United States
89142LV00002BA